The Silence
Between Us

The Silence Between Us

Selected Haiku of Wally Swist

edited by

Randy M. Brooks

Christine Sandidge
Student Editor

Brooks Books
Decatur, Illinois

Printed in the United States of America

First Edition

ISBN: 1-929820-07-0

Brooks Books
3720 N. Woodridge Drive
Decatur, Illinois 62526

www.brooksbookshaiku.com
brooksbooks@sbcglobal.net

for

Paris Finley and Linda Jones

Publication Credits

Grateful acknowledgment is made to the editors of the following publications in which some of these poems appeared in present or earlier versions:

Albatross (Romania), *American Haiku* (Modern American Literature: New Approaches) (Peter Lang, Inc., 2003), *Blowing Reeds* (Timberline Press, 1995), *Brussels Sprout, Chimney Smoke* (Juniper Press, 1988), *Frogpond, The Gristmill's Trough* (Hummingbird Press, 1991), *Haiku: Poetry Ancient and Modern* (Tuttle Publishing/MQ Editions, 2002), *The Haiku Anthology* (W. W. Norton & Company, Inc., 1999), *Haiku Moment* (Charles E. Tuttle Company, Inc., 1993), *A Haiku Path* (Haiku Society of America, 1994), *Haiku sans frontieres: une anthologie mondiale* (Les Editions David, 1998), *Haiku Seasons* (Kodansha International, 1996), *High/Coo, Hummingbird,* Mad River Press Broadside (#9), *Mayfly, Modern Haiku, The Mown Meadow: First Selected Haiku & Sequences, 1977-1994* (Los Hombres Press, 1996), *Persimmon, Place of the Long River: A Connecticut River Anthology* (Blue Moon Press, 1995), *Raw Nervz, The Red Moon Anthology* (Red Moon Press, 1996/1997), *Sparrow* (#58), *Sugaring Buckets* (High/Coo Press, 1989), *Train Whistle* (Proof Press, 1996), *Unmarked Stones* (Burnt Lake Press, 1988), *The White Rose* (Timberline Press, 2000), and *Wind Chimes.*

Publishers' Note

Brooks Books is pleased to publish *The Silence Between Us: Selected Haiku of Wally Swist*. Wally Swist has been an active contributor to the American haiku community since the 1970s, publishing haiku in numerous haiku magazines and serving as book review editor for *Modern Haiku* magazine from 1989 until 1997.

Several chapbooks of his haiku have been published over the last fifteen years, and he has four books of lyric or narrative poetry in print. His haiku have been included in several major haiku anthologies and published in many magazines, so it is with great pleasure that Brooks Books publishes a gathering of Wally Swist's best haiku into this collection, *The Silence Between Us*.

Special thanks are due to Lee Gurga, editor of *Modern Haiku* magazine, who helped Wally review his published work and select haiku for inclusion in this collection. We also reconsidered the manuscript selection and added haiku. Wally has carefully arranged the order of the haiku so that the reader enjoys a careful slow read, without jarring or unfortunate juxtapositions of haiku.

Wally Swist is a master of nature haiku, and he brings a certain reserved New England understatement to his work. It is often the things unsaid, the silences between the images, that make all the difference in his work. We are sure you will enjoy this journey into the "silence" as you read and savor each haiku in this book.

—Randy & Shirley Brooks
Decatur, Illinois

Author's Acknowledgment

I am indebted to many individuals in the North American haiku community for their encouragement since I began practicing my writing of haiku in 1973.

I offer my continued gratitude to Randy and Shirley Brooks, who offered constructive criticism of some of my early attempts in the genre, when they published the magazine, *High/Coo*, in the mid-to-late seventies. I must also mention the support that the late Elizabeth Searle Lamb offered when she was editor of *Frogpond* through many years.

One of my finest memories is when, during the New York Small Press Book Fair in 1995, Cor van den Heuvel happened to walk up to a table where I was helping my friend, Gary Metras of Adastra Press, and introduced himself, vis-a-vis my nametag. I will always cherish what Cor had to say about my work, and that he was planning to use some of my haiku in a new edition of *The Haiku Anthology*.

I need to thank Dorothy Howard, of Proof Press in Quebec, for initially inviting me to submit haiku of mine, and for republishing my work long after I had submitted any new work to her.

I offer my appreciation to Lee Gurga, who for so many years has provided inspiration, not only through his own haiku, but also through what has always been a felicitious exchange of friendship through the mail.

Lastly, I would be remiss in not mentioning my mentor, the late Robert Spiess, who I was in correspondence with from January 1976 until two weeks before his death in March 2001.

I find it necessary to offer my gratitude "to the land," and my good fortune to have lived where I have. For twelve years, I resided in an apartment of a refurbished barn in Cushman, Massachusetts, whose property abuts a preserved wetlands, "Haskins' Flats," near the Leverett town line.

The effect of my years there are not dissimilar to what John Wills found by living on "Sweetwater," his farm in Tennessee, where he wrote some of his finest haiku. "The land," for me, was, and is to this day, a living inspiration of what Raymond Roseliep termed the "haiku moment" to be, as "a peephole to the absolute." In light of this, it may well be apropos that I chose one of the lines in my haiku dedicated to Roseliep to be the title of this collection.

I am grateful to the Robert Francis Trust for poetry residencies at Fort Juniper in the autumn of 1998 and from September 2003 to September 2005 where this book was "finished." Also, I am appreciative of the support of the Connecticut Commission on the Arts in awarding me an individual artist's grant in 2003 "for poetic recognition" that offered assistance in completing this collection.

The meadows, brooks, and local mountains of the Pioneer Valley in Western Massachusetts opened themselves to me in a perpetuity in those years, and I continue to find a blessing and healing in the natural world that has only deepened since then.

How timely it is for me to have returned to this land, just a few miles over the ridge where I had lived, after some years of living in a city, and to begin to practice my sense of place again, anew.

In keeping with this, it is my wish to share a sense of wonder in both the natural world and in human nature. May the following pages offer a discovery of the epiphany in the commonplace for us all.

—*Wally Swist*
Fort Juniper
The Robert Francis Homestead
Cushman, Massachusetts

Table of Contents

Author's Preface: The Poetics of Walking

Haiku is a poetic genre that can be defined as the juxtaposition of two or more images that provides insight into nature or human nature. It does not, necessarily, need to be written in lines of five, seven, and five syllables, as it often is in Japan, where haiku poetry originated. There is no exact definition of the English "syllable" in Japanese, except for *onji*, "sound-signs" or "sound-symbols." Also, "syllables" in Japanese are shorter than they are in English. So, seventeen syllables in English can be tediously lengthy in Japanese. The essence of a successful haiku itself is in the experience of an eternal moment, the numinous found in nature, and in the austerity of the juxaposition of the images themselves, in that experience, without the use of metaphor or simile.

Haiku for me has been a path, a way of life, a vehicle through which I see the world anew daily and newly many times during the day. For me it has meant to learn how to *look*, and to paraphrase the American lyric poet Mary Oliver: "the more you look, the more you find." For instance, when I find the first starflower of the season in early May, blooming, as always, beside Canada mayflower, my eyes range up the slope. And I see another and another. It is in this opening of vision that the best haiku are created.

Haiku is a poetry of consciousness: the tones of Bashô's temple bell dissolving among the peonies in the garden, and the resonance of that tolling emanating in the flowers themselves. Haiku is also a poetic, and spiritual, discipline of discovering the epiphany in the commonplace. Since nature, and often human nature, is found outside the walls of our homes and in the outer world, the poetics of haiku, for me, has always meant walking out into nature and having the natural world move through me.

Walking facilitates a kind of psychic *feng-shui*. Either strolling into a sunlit meadow or hiking a trail up a mountain in the rain, in this "activity of non-action" there is a relinquishing of ego. One's will dissolves into divine will. There is not just the sense, but the experience, of: *all is one*, as the medical intuitive Caroline Myss often recounts in her work regarding healing in relationship to the system of the chakras of our bodies.

It is in walking that the best haiku can be created. The eminent haiku poet Bashô walked his *Narrow Road to the Deep North*, and several other poets and writers, practicing in other genres, have too. The Russian poet Vladimir Mayakovsky wrote about this in his book *How Verses Are Made*.

When working out the rhythm and music of one of his poems, Mayakovsky would recite the lines of his poem in his mind as he walked the streets of Moscow. The pace of his strides over the cobblestones was in concord to the integral harmony of the poem's evolving of and within itself. The mechanics of the poem would resolve itself through the rhythm of his walking.

In Henry David Thoreau's essay, *On Walking*, that remains contemporary through his transcendental use of language, he compares the rhythm of his "strolling" to the equanimity of his life and all of what he experiences in the natural world around him.

The poet Mary Oliver is said to squirrel pencils in the crevasses of various limbs of trees on her favorite walks. How delightful it is to create one's own serendipity.

The poetics of my own poetry originate in this manner. Over many years, it is in the manner of learning the names of the flora and fauna that present themselves in such an array through each of the seasons on my walks. In this knowledge of being able to name what I see in the natural world precipitates the language in the poems that open themselves to me.

The distinguished mythologist and expert in comparative religion, Joseph Campbell, often referred to the Sioux shaman, Black Elk, and his concept of "Sacred Mountain." Campbell speaks eloquently about that "particular" mountain, and that it need not be the tallest peak in the world, but he refers to it as a "power spot," somewhere you can "look" over the plains. It is a place in nature where you experience oneness with the earth, and refresh yourself with renewed vision.

My "Sacred Mountain," not to mention other "power spots" in and around Amherst, Massachusetts, is Mount Toby, located in nearby Sunderland. Mount Toby is enveloped in a lushness of hardwoods and ferns, and I have seen deer, bear, and porcupine cross its trails.

From the fire tower at the summit, only 1,240 feet at the peak, look north. On a clear day: at two o'clock, you can see Mount Monadnock's granite dome in New Hampshire; at eleven o'clock, Mount Snow's jagged peak is prominent in Vermont; and due west, Mount Greylock's rounded protrusion expresses itself in the distance in the Berkshires, bordering New York's easternmost state line.

It is not only in language that we create a poetics, but through our interaction with nature and its beneficence. It is in looking and looking, then seeing, that we experience what is epiphanal in the commonplace.

Whether it is Bashô's travail on his *Narrow Road*, and through his ardor, his opening to the nature around him, or Mayakovsky's working out the rhythms and word-choice in his poems. Whether it is Thoreau's "strolling" to become in touch with himself and in nature itself, or Mary Oliver, like a Johnny Apple-Seed, gifting herself with pencils in the narrows of trees. It is the poetics of walking and *seeing* that allow us to participate in what can be termed as the *ah-ness* of the "haiku moment."

—*Wally Swist*

Holes in Our Preconceptions: The Haiku of Wally Swist

Wally Swist's heart is in old books, but his soul is in haiku. He is an antiquarian bookseller by profession, a poet by necessity. Over the past 15 years, Swist has produced a fine body of haiku, arguably as fine as those written by anyone else writing in English. His haiku moments are sympathetically apprehended and precisely drawn. Swist then goes one step further, engaging all the tools of Western poetics to produce haiku that are memorable as poems, experiences in themselves. This collection presents a wide range of haiku and senryu: haiku in which we find peace in the scent of pine needles, haiku with exuberance and lightness, haiku that engage haiku traditions, both Japanese and American.

In Swist's haiku, the cycle of the seasons touches the cycle of our lives and both are altered by the interaction. We find our mental perambulations reflected in a spiral of rose petals, not merely as a symbol, but as a sympathy between our human cares and the world around us. The log sweats with the logger. The waterfall entices the couple to roar with it. The dove's call and response is felt in the (coo)lness of our skin. Sparrows mate as dandelion embryos drift on the breeze. We feel the roan's breath. Unlike many so-called haiku today, these are the haiku of a poet touched by seasonal consciousness while living life honestly and directly. Swist's haiku have a materiality without materialism.

Epiphanies tinged with mystery are found in the most unlikely places: in the black spots on the cow, the sunburn on our neck, feathers on the pond. Scientists say that we get over eighty percent of our sensory information from our eyes; it is not surprising that haiku with visual images are the most common. We find them here, but we also find the tingle of other senses. Long-time *Modern Haiku* editor Robert Spiess observed that the most memorable haiku were made up of multiple sense images. You should not be surprised to find many such haiku here.

There are exuberances here, but they are understated in the haiku way. These haiku start us moving, then tip us into wonder with a breath. The lightness of haiku is not the lightness of light verse, but the deftness of a master who defines the silence before and after with a single note or suggests a range of mountains with a brushstroke.

While focused on the poet's life in nature, there is also a cast of interesting characters in these poems: a bartender, a laborer, a hospice patient, a street sweeper. Together they move with Swist through village and meadow.

Swist is the poet's haiku poet. The best haiku use literal images to share moments of wonder, then go beyond mere factual reporting, beyond "nature notes" to genuine word experiences. Poets who use startling words in haiku often fail by moving the center of gravity outside the experience of the poem and into the realm of the intellect. The best haiku say, "Look at this!" rather than, "Look at me!" Swist's word choices can be startling, but never overdone; he balances on the razor's edge between epiphany and oxymoron to enhance our experience of the poem while staying true to the moment. This ability to use words in an original yet vital way is perhaps what separates Swist most strikingly from most poets writing haiku today. In this collection you will find the ratchet of the cricket, the snarl of a dog's chain, a snake roping through tall grass and other wonders of Swist's poetic mind.

Swist not only honors the moment, but also honors his forebears in haiku. Two of his haiku could be seen as direct responses to haiku of Bashô, Japan's most revered classical haiku poet. Here is one of Bashô's famous haiku:

> on a withered branch
> a crow has perched—
> autumn evening

Bashô's is a vivid, classic moment. An impression of an autumn evening filled with mystery and pathos. Swist's is more active:

early autumn evening
    crows standing
among the stones of the field

His "early" gives us the changing light more directly, animating the otherwise lifeless stones. Swist's crows have the same impenetrable blackness of Bashô's, yet we are made aware that in spite of their somber symbolism, they are also the "birds of the field" that Christ reminded us to consider. The stones reappear in another haiku:

stones in the sunlit meadow . . .
    pierced by the shrill drone
of cicadas

Swist's haiku makes us feel the stillness of the day without describing it explicitly as Bashô does:

So still:
it pierces the rocks
cicadas' cry

Swist also honors his roots in American haiku, dedicating haiku to some of the masters of the first generation of American haiku poets, including Nicholas Virgilio, Charles Dickson, Geraldine Clinton Little, Raymond Roseliep, and John Wills. The haiku of Virgilio's that has inspired Swist makes us cold and colder, deepening the mood as we sink with the kittens in the dark water:

the sack of kittens
sinking in the icy creek,
increases the cold

Swist's water is icy but surprisingly inviting:

bracing the chill
    moonlight rushes
in the icy river

As Swist feels the dew through the hole in his shoe, these haiku let the world in by making holes in our preconceptions. Rock with the hayrack—or with the retarded boy listening to his Walkman. Lean against the fence with the left over Christmas trees. Discover with Swist the unmarked stones in the Quaker graveyard. Drop your personality, drop your persona, and discover Swist's world of grace. Swist has written some fine haiku that no one else could have written. Sit back and enjoy them. They are poems that are at home in any part of North America east of the Mississippi, and, I suspect, in many other places as well. Enjoy them as a celebration of life, of haiku, and of the work of visionaries such as R. H. Blyth and Robert Spiess who cultivated the American soil so that these poems could bear fruit.

—Lee Gurga
Lincoln, Illinois

Selected Haiku

we wake at dawn
crow calling crow
through the fog

at the stop light
in separate cars
we yawn together

spring mist
Japanese silk
on her breasts

cool morning of dew—
cutting radishes
for my wife's lunch

silence after our argument
    crumpled cigarette pack
uncurling

winter sunset:
in the brass door handle
an eviction notice

Christmas day:
at peace
peeling potatoes

tugging the snarl
out of its chain—
neighbor's watchdog

one unbroken pane
remaining in the shed
full moon

talk about integrity
    rain running off
our umbrellas

Quaker graves
in a clearing
unmarked stones

at the edge
of the iced-over pond—
a burst of cattails

dropping a handful of change
at the toll booth
a missing child poster

windy morning:
a retarded man
rolls his head

that patch of snow
the widow considered shoveling
smaller now

along the path
to the peace pagoda
fragrance of pine

the long winter over—
three pennies in my coat
for *I Ching*

going over and over
what my wife said—
petals of the rose

chimney smoke
graying the twilight—
our conversation deepens

stopping in my steps:
a bird who seems to know me
calls from pines

dewy morning:
the logging truck's load
sweating sap

above the roar of the rapids
    my wife and I call
rock to rock

mourning dove
answers mourning dove—
coolness after the rain

a white mare grazes
in a grove of birch—
thunderheads

row after row of radishes
      each top shivering
in the cool rain

a sparrow
tries to mount a mate
dandelion gone to seed

the azalea opens
one flower, then two—
we make up

pelting rain
the cow's black spots
move through mist

farm banter
the bartender chalks
her pool cue

trail of summer wind
    fawn follows doe
through meadow grass

sunburn . . .
twilight along
the ridge

October twilight:
old man sweeping
the empty parking lot

cordwood split
    wedge
of geese

field of frost
    the open
milkweed pod

duck feathers
on the pond . . .
snow falling

flurries . . .
making sour cream-potato soup
to Brahms

bend of the brook
    fox prints
etched in ice

ice melting
the drum
of the sugaring buckets

cluster of dandelions
    a yellow rim
in the grackle's eyes

courting again . . .
a flicker hammers
the oak's dead limbs

dew in meadow grass
a swallowtail drifts
among stellaria

shining in the heat
the laborer's back
sticky with sweat

stars gather
in the gristmill's trough
water wheel creaking

late summer coolness
dew soaks into
holes in my shoes

October rain
breath smokes from
the roan's nostrils

new moon
tightening the darkness
a cricket's ratchet

junco rustling
the milkweed husk—
bitter winter wind

the farther into it,
the farther it moves away—
spring mist

crow carcass
cleaned to the bones
the feathers fluttering

spring freshet—
a mallard coaxes
her ducklings

heavy morning dew—
whitetail deer scatter
mist in the meadow

sunny hollow—
the startled black snake
ropes through tall grass

sky dark with rain
    wasps curled in slats
of the wooden porch boards

new buds
the ferris wheel
takes another turn

April morning
    spring
in the robin's hop

bend after bend
    trail stones
silvered with rain

towhee's song—
the smell of drying dew
across the meadow

deep bend of the brook
    the kingfisher's chatter
after its dive

summer drizzle
sulphur butterflies flutter
through crimson clover

joe-pye weed
silhouetted in the sunset—
the heat

a song for every direction
    mockingbird atop
the weathervane

heat haze
the beat
of a dragonfly's wings

cool scent at dusk—
foraging the hayed meadow's rim
a spotted doe

goldfinches emerge
from the raspberry thicket
summer dusk

centering sunlight
    the orb weaver
spins its web

thunderheads . . .
the glow of the meadow
fringed with goldenrod

checking the herd—
the roving sheep dog's
blind eye

fog rolls across the meadow
    wave after wave
pulsating with crickets

first tinge of color in the ash
    snakeskin in the sand
beside the pond

far into twilight
milkweed seeds cross the meadow—
the evening star

blue autumn evening
a maple's orange-going-to-red
flares in the pond

the flatbed of baled hay
rocks with the tractor's pull
Indian summer

that one bird
with a hinge in its voice
creaks in the wind

roar of the brook—
brown oak leaves drift
down through the rain

out of the blowing reeds
and swirling mist
voices of geese

the sound of sleet
    a mouse gnaws
inside the closet wall

Christmas eve
leaning against the chain-link fence
the trees no one wanted

bitter cold:
the steeple clock's hands
have stopped

mounded snow
the swallow's nest
reveals itself

new snow
the cottontail
licks its paws

the insistent voice
of a black-capped chickadee
snowy morning

curving over the plunge pool
    snow-covered arc
of the fallen alder

plummeting
into a silent pool
the frozen waterfall

bracing the chill
    moonlight rushes
in the icy river

for Nicholas A. Virgilio

dawn mists rise . . .
the river bottom covered
with mud-caked stones

casting into a pool
from the center of himself
fly fisherman

fanning out
in the boat's wake
day's end

moving
through mist
mute swans

mountain laurel blossoms
    a luminous moth ascends
into moonlight

for Charles R. Dickson

heat lightning
the screams
of mating raccoons

soothing rain:
the mown meadow releases
pungence of mint

morning star
the hospice patient
lingers

heat haze
windrows of cut hay
blanket the hills

wave after wave of peepers
    coolness blowing through
the rolling fog

freight train whistling—
the wind nudges umbels
of Queen Anne's lace

streaked dawn sky—
goldfinches spread out
through purple loosestrife

early autumn evening
    crows standing
among the stones of the field

scraping across snow
    the unlocked gate
glazed with ice

letting go
of my disappointments
first night of peepers

shaded from sunlight—
an open book airs beside
the sickroom window

redemption center squabble
    a homeless man recounts
his stack of cans

new age bookstore
guessing at
people's past lives

one strand of mist then the mountain

intensive care—
the checkered linoleum
changing patterns

sharing my good news
    his handshake
slackens

summer dawn—
the street sweeper's bristles
scraping the sidewalk

stifling heat—
the pond caked
with green scum

stones in the sunlit meadow . . .
    pierced by the shrill drone
of cicadas

autumn chill—
unwrapping a moth from the folds
of my blanket

finding time
on a broken parking meter . . .
autumn rain

dusk—
the rumble of a farm wagon
piled high with pumpkins

buzz of silence—
the apiary submerged beneath
hives of snow

shadows
down the snowy slope . . .
a coyote's gleaming eyes

dusk lights the ridge
evening grosbeaks pinwheel
tree to tree

night sky filled with clouds
    the trill of one peeper
higher than the rest

streaming beneath the new green reeds
    the rippling flag
of a tadpole's tail

silencing the peepers
in a single wave—
my shadow in the sedge

mountain trail . . .
the fragrance of horses
mingling with pine

plowing
a broken pine twig—
the snail's proud horns

the sky black with rain—
crows in free fall
fighting over the rookery

spring rain—
an ancient pattern gleaming
on the turtle's shell

twilight coolness—
    a glow of new leaves
fading from the last of the hills

Easter Sunday:
    a farmer's spade gleams
in the loosened darkness of earth

dusk fading . . .
straggling geese in silhouette
trumpet their return

mourning cloak ascending the trail—
. . . stone to stone
and shadow to shadow

for Geraldine Clinton Little

rain sprinkles the river—
pollen yellows the funnel
of a trout swirl

trembling larva—
trout bubbles on the brook's surface
finally break

mountain summit—
the path through the pines
redolent with resin

all the way
down the mountainside—
a coolness from ledge to ledge

a ray of sunlight
grazes the road's shoulder—
orange hawkweed

deep twilight—
the abandoned horse pasture
thick with buttercups

a red ant crawls along
spines of the purple thistle—
the heat

humming to myself—
a hovering dragonfly
ruffles the air

dry mountain streambed:
    a red admiral settles
on the dusty rock

for Robert Spiess

lazy afternoon—
a chickadee answers the calls
on my bird tape

illuminating
the silence between us . . .
firefly

for Raymond Roseliep

storm clouds approaching . . .
    pointed purple folds
of the bearded iris

lightning flash—
the wind in the trees
fills with rain

crossing the field
of moonlit potato flowers . . .
drifting cloud shadow

honeycombed by termites—
the deadfall breaks up
into a musty odor

opening into forest
on rusted hinges—
the old pasture gate

daybreak—
a full moon sets above
the frosted meadow

for John Wills

closed mental hospital
swings creaking
among windblown weeds

a cricket's rasp—
dusk collecting at the roots
of the dry corn stalks

sudden rainstorm—
crimson leaves stick
to our new umbrellas

harvest moon—
silently, the retarded boy
rocks to his walkman

rainy autumn night—
    the shop owner works
the beads of his abacus

November twilight:
the mountainside of birches
lavender with shadow

roadside farm stand—
a child inhales the fragrance
of baskets of apples

first snow . . .
knowing by the hush
before raising the blinds

bittersweet tangled
in a grove of staghorn sumac—
winter sunrise

snow flurrying—
the milkweed pod releases
a stream of seeds

the silence
between bells . . .
snow falling

waking up—
    my cuffs still wet
from a walk in new snow

for Bob Arnold

moving off the trail
in pairs through the snow:
frozen coyote tracks

the starling's whistle—
changing places between clothespins
frozen to the line

glittering along the trail
in half-melted snow—
fractured mica crystals

dry season:
the mountain fire tower
crackles with static

sweltering dusk . . .
suspended dandelion seeds
gather in a cluster

waves of shimmering heat . . .
  the sun-bleached rocks
of the dry mountain stream

summer pasture—
  a child emerges
in the old man's eyes

crickets echoing . . .
  knots in the wood
of the new pine porch

gray autumn dawn:
the thorny thicket of rose hips
glistens with frost

shimmer of the moon—
swirling wind scours the frozen pond
with roadside sand

the red-tailed hawk's glide—
    quiet growing among
the snowy pines

About the Author

Wally Swist was born in New Haven, Connecticut in 1953. His haiku have appeared in many periodicals devoted to the genre, including *Frogpond, Mayfly,* and *Modern Haiku.* Also, he served as book review editor for *Modern Haiku* from 1989 until 1997.

His longer lyric and short narrative poems have appeared in *Alaska Quarterly Review, Appalachia, The Anthology of Magazine Verse and Yearbook of American Poetry* (1995-1996) (Monitor Book Company, Inc., 1997), *Connecticut Review, Sanctuary: The Massachusetts Audubon Magazine, Osiris, Puckerbrush Review, Stories from Where We Live: The North Atlantic Coast* (Milkweed Editions, 2000), *Stories from Where We Live: The Eastern Woodlands* (Milkweed Editions, 2005), and *Yankee.*

Sahara: A Journal of New England Poetry published a special issue devoted to Swist's work in the winter of 2003 that featured many of his new and recent poems and a typescript recorded interview regarding his craft and life as a writer.

A lecture he delivered in the Robert Frost Homestead 2002 Literary Series, entitled "The Friendship of Robert Frost and Robert Francis: High Pressure Weather and Country Air," was published in the Summer 2003 issue of *Puckerbrush Review.*

In August 2003, he gave the finale reading in the Sunken Garden Poetry Festival, accompanied by jazz cellist, Eugene Friesen, a member of Paul Winter Consort. One of the poems he read that evening was broadcast nationally on *NPR's Saturday Weekend Edition*.

Twice he has been awarded grants in poetry from the Connecticut Commission on the Arts, in 1978 and in 2003. He has also been awarded two writing residencies at Fort Juniper, the Robert Francis Homestead, in Amherst, Massachusetts, in the autumn of 1998, and for two full years from September 2003 to September 2005.

He is the General Book Manager at the University Store at the University of Massachusetts, Amherst.

Books By Wally Swist

Veils of the Divine, Newtown, CT: Hanover Press, 2003, 84pp., $12.00, quality trade paperback.

The New Life, West Hartford, CT: Plinth Books, 1998, 80pp., $12.00, quality trade paperback, $24.00, cloth.

The Mown Meadow, San Diego, CA: Los Hombres Press, 1996, 80pp., $9.95, quality trade paperback.

For the Dance, Easthampton, MA: Adastra Press, 1991, 45pp., letterpress, $8.00, paperback, $25.00, handbound, cloth over boards.

Chapbooks By Wally Swist

The White Rose, Fulton, MO: Timberline Press, 2000, 40pp., letterpress, $7.50, paperback.

Train Whistle, Aylmer, Quebec, Canada,: Proof Press, 1996, 40pp., $5.00, wraps.

Blowing Reeds, Fulton, MO: Timberline Press, 1995, 28pp., letterpress, paperback.

The Gristmill's Trough, Richland Center, WI: Hummingbird Press, 1991, 12pp., $5.00, wraps.

Sugaring Buckets, Battleground, IN: High/Coo Press, 1989, 20pp., $2.00, wraps, $10.00, handbound, cloth over boards.

Unmarked Stones, Sherbrooke, Quebec, Canada: Burnt Lake Press, 1988, 36pp., letterpress, $5.00, paperback.

Chimney Smoke, La Crosse, WI: Juniper Press, 1988, 12pp., letterpress, $4.00, wraps.

Waking Up the Ducks, Easthampton, MA: Adastra Press, 1987, 18pp., letterpress, $5.00, paperback.

Of What We're Given, Guilford, CT: Dunk Rock Books, 1980, 35pp., $5.00, wraps.

Magazine Appearances

Over sixty magazine appearances, including:

Alaska Quarterly Review

America: The National Catholic Weekly

Appalachia

Connecticut Review

The Larcom Review: A Journal of the Arts and Literature of New England

Longhouse

Northern New England Review

Old Crow

Osiris

Outerbridge

Painted Bride Quarterly

Poet Lore

Poetry East

Puckerbrush Review

Rolling Stone

Sahara: A Journal of New England Poetry

Sanctuary: The Massachusetts Audubon Magazine

Snowy Egret

Telephone

The Yale Literary Magazine

Yankee

Anthology Appearances

The Anthology of Magazine Verse and Yearbook of American Poetry 1995-1996 (Monitor Book Company, Inc., 1997)

The Duchess of Malfi's Apricots & Other Literary Fruits (University of South Carolina Press, 2002)

The Haiku Anthology (W. W. Norton & Company, Inc., 1999)

Haiku Moment (Charles E. Tuttle & Company, Inc., 1993)

Haiku: Poetry Ancient and Modern (Tuttle Publishing/MQ Editions, 2002)

Haiku sans frontieres: une anthologie mondiale (Les Editions David, 1998)

Haiku World: An International Poetry Almanac (Kodansha International, 1996)

Intimate Kisses: The Poetry of Sexual Love (New World Library, 2001)

Place of the Long River: A Connecticut River Anthology (Blue Moon Press, 1995)

Proposing on the Brooklyn Bridge: Poems about Marriage (Poetworks/Grayson Books, 2003)

Stories from Where We Live: The North Atlantic Coast (Milkweed Editions, 2000)

Stories from Where We Live: The Eastern Woodlands (Milkweed Editions, 2005)

Teaching & Workshop Experience

Mentor for *Night of Fresh Voices,* Sunken Garden Poetry Festival, Hill-Stead Museum, Farmington, CT, 2001-2003. State of Connecticut Poetry-in-the-Schools Program, Hillhouse High School, New Haven, CT and The Wadsworth Atheneum, Hartford, CT, 1979/1980. YWCA, Poetry Workshop, New Haven, CT, 1977.

Writing Residency

The Robert Francis Homestead, Fort Juniper, Cushman, MA, autumn 1998 and September 2003 to September 2005.

Grants/Awards

Connecticut Commission on the Arts Grant in Poetry, 1978 and 2003.

Guest Lecture

"The Friendship of Robert Frost and Robert Francis: High-pressure Weather and Country Air," The Frost Farm, Derry, NH, August 11, 2002.

Featured Readings

The Sunken Garden Poetry Festival, Hill-Stead Museum, Farmington, CT, August 2003

Hartford Public Library Broadside Series, Hartford, CT, April 2003

Valentine's Prelude, Benefit Reading for the Sunken Garden Poetry Festival, Makeshift Theatre, Hill-Stead Museum, Farmington, CT, February 2001

Trinity College (Sponsored by the English Department), Hartford, CT, October 2001

Cheney Hall Broadside Series, Glastonbury, CT, May 2000

Buttonwood Tree, Middletown, CT, March 2000

UCONN Co-Op Bookstore, Storrs, CT, November 1999

Booklink Booksellers (Thorne's Marketplace), Northampton, MA, October 1998

The Amherst Book and Plow Festival, Amherst, MA, June 1997

The Odyssey Bookshop, South Hadley, MA, October 1993

Wootton's Books, Amherst, MA, October 1991 and October 1995

Readers & Writers Live, Northampton Center for the Arts (Sponsored by the Globe Bookshop), Northampton, MA, February 1988 and March 1992

The Saint Mark's Poetry Project, New York, NY, March 1980

Yale Poetry Weekend, Yale University Art Gallery, New Haven, CT, January 1979

and other bookstores, colleges, universities, and poetry festivals.